One Belfast Boy

One Belfast Boy

Patricia McMahon

Photographs by

Alan O'Connor

Houghton Mifflin Company
Boston 1999

Text copyright © 1999 by Patricia McMahon
Photographs copyright © 1999 by Alan O'Connor

This book is set in Electra and Mason Sans.
Book design by Lisa Diercks

Library of Congress Cataloging-in-Publication Data

McMahon, Patricia.
One Belfast boy / Patricia McMahon ; photographs by Alan O'Connor.
p. cm.
Summary: Describes the life of Liam Leathem, a young Catholic boy,
and his family as he prepares for a boxing match that he sees as
the first step out of violence-plagued Belfast.
ISBN 0-395-68620-2
1. Belfast (Northern Ireland)—Social life and customs—Juvenile literature.
2. Catholics—Northern Ireland—Belfast—Juvenile literature. 3. Family—Northern
Ireland—Belfast—Juvenile literature. 4. Boys—Northern Ireland—Belfast—Juvenile
literature. [1. Belfast (Northern Ireland)—Social conditions. 2. Catholics—
Northern Ireland—Belfast. 3. Family life—Northern Ireland—Belfast.]
I. O'Connor, Alan (Alan Patrick), ill.   II. Title.
DA995.B5M29   1999
306'.09416'7—dc21   98-28568 CIP AC

Printed in Hong Kong
DNP 10 9 8 7 6 5 4 3 2 1

This book is dedicated to
my father, James G. McMahon,
lover of the words, the music, the ancient airs;
and to the memory of my mother,
Janet McMahon,
who was born a McMullin,
who was gone too soon,
and who told me to write.
Even now, I would wish you one more day to stay.
— P. McM.

To Mum, Dad, Av, Noders, and Officer Dibble—
onward and upward . . .
— A. O'C.

Acknowledgments

I wish to express my complete and utter thanks to the Leathem family—Peter, Bridie, Peter Jr., Michael, and, of course, Liam—who were generous with their hospitality and more than lived up to Peter's promise to "make us more than welcome." They could not have been kinder if they tried; they kept the tea and the talk going.

Mickey Hawkins was instrumental in the success of our time in Belfast. I thank him for his introduction to the Leathem family, for his patience in explicating some basic facts of boxing, for opening the doors of the club so wide with welcome. I would like to thank Tony Leonard as well, and Damien Kelly, Brian Magee, and all the boxers, young and old, in the Holy Trinity Boxing Club.

I had a grand time all in all at the Holy Trinity Boys School, and for that I am grateful to Mr. Basil Hutton, principal, and to all the faculty and staff—most particularly to Mr. Gerry Armstrong and his seventh-form class, who are great lads all and better actors still.

To Milo and Edna Butler and their clan—Grattan, Daniel (the songwriter), Fintan, and Maureen—I wish to say thank you for conversation, strong tea, Irish poetry, and a lovely argumentative drive to Dublin.

I wish to thank Alan O'Connor and Debbie Cassidy for giving the stranger bed and board and to thank Alan for his hard work and good company. I have Michael O'Brien of O'Brien Press, Dublin, to thank for suggesting I work with Alan. And I thank Tom and Sheila O'Connor for their generous Dublin welcome as well.

As always, I thank Karen Klockner and Kim Keller. George Nicholson has my gratitude for his encouragement and enthu-

siasm on this book. The work of Robbie Frost of Houston, Texas, was of great importance and I thank him and his pals Rudy and Bruno. On more than one occasion, Jane Stilley came to the rescue, as did Judy Staley, so to both of them I am truly grateful. Jackie Cook and Hasha Baker aided me on my journey, and Mary McMahon saved the day. I thank her with love. The same goes, as always, to my two McCarthys who watch me go, wait, and worry—"Ye are both so fine to me."

— P. McM.

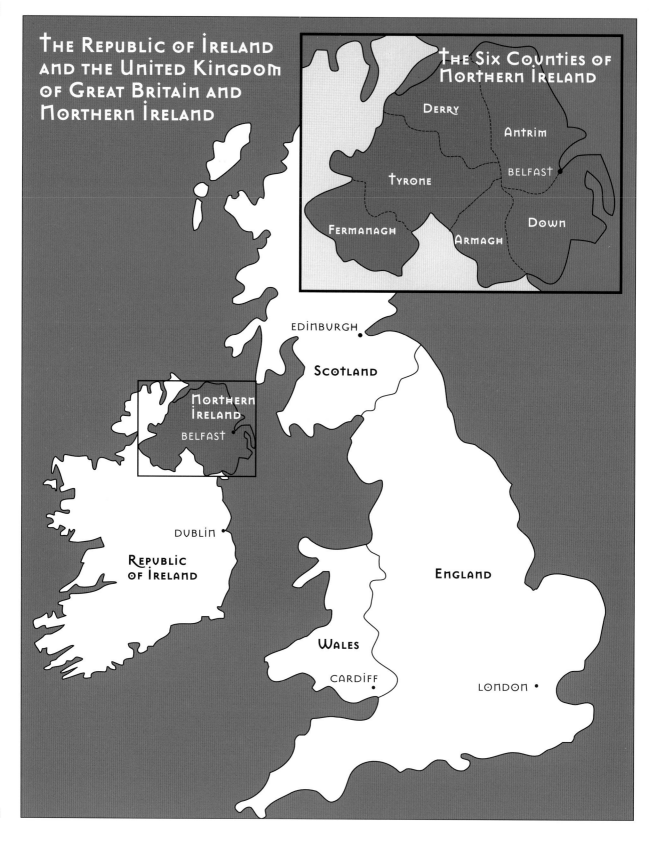

THE REPUBLIC OF İRELAND AND THE UNITED KINGDOM OF GREAT BRITAIN AND NORTHERN İRELAND

THE SIX COUNTIES OF NORTHERN İRELAND

DERRY

ANTRIM

BELFAST

TYRONE

FERMANAGH

ARMAGH

DOWN

EDINBURGH

SCOTLAND

NORTHERN İRELAND

BELFAST

DUBLIN

REPUBLIC OF İRELAND

ENGLAND

WALES

CARDIFF

LONDON

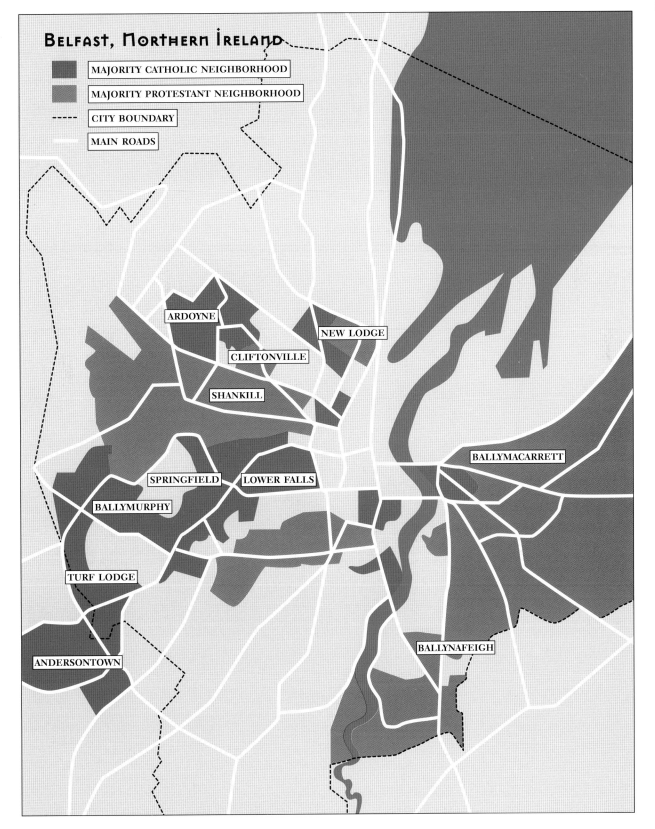

BELFAST, NORTHERN IRELAND

- ■ MAJORITY CATHOLIC NEIGHBORHOOD
- ■ MAJORITY PROTESTANT NEIGHBORHOOD
- ---- CITY BOUNDARY
- —— MAIN ROADS

ARDOYNE

NEW LODGE

CLIFTONVILLE

SHANKILL

BALLYMACARRETT

SPRINGFIELD   LOWER FALLS

BALLYMURPHY

TURF LODGE

BALLYNAFEIGH

ANDERSONTOWN

An Old Story

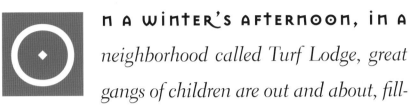 n a winter's afternoon, in a neighborhood called Turf Lodge, great gangs of children are out and about, filling the streets. Rocks bounce against a wall painted with words as a small girl climbs to the top of it. A boy walks past the rock throwers. The girl calls out the boy's name, but he keeps walking. Some bigger boys, hands cupped around cigarettes, stand waiting—waiting for they know not what. They, too, call out the boy's name.

The younger ones begin to sing out a song they all know. "What about Ulster?" they sing. "What about Sinn Fein?"

Nearby, a group of soldiers, dressed and ready for battle, walks down a similar street. With their long guns held high, they look at everyone down the rifle sights. A small boy runs

from his home, shooting a plastic gun at them. A dog turns his head away, uninterested in what he sees every day.

Not much farther away, an armored truck, gray as the winter light, hurries down a rubbish-strewn street. The truck stops under a lamppost marked IRA in big letters, the same as all the other posts on the street. Soldiers spill out the back of the truck to investigate: a bomb has been reported. A group of long-haired and freckled girls runs toward the soldiers, shouting unkind words as the armed men begin to search the neighborhood.

At the end of the street, a soccer game goes on and the kids ignore the fuss, for it is nothing new. A wall some twenty feet high rises behind them. Nearby a door is painted with the words BRITS OUT, and on a building there is a large mural of a soldier with a giant red line painted over him.

On the other side of the wall, children are also playing soccer. The curbs of their street are painted red, white, and blue. The lampposts display the flag of Great Britain—red, white, and blue. On their side of the wall are written the words NO SURRENDER.

The soccer players have never seen one another, although they can hear over the wall. The peace wall, as it is known, does its job of keeping people apart. The children have never met, they probably never will. If they did, there's every good chance a fight would begin.

3

This is the city of Belfast, in a place known as Ulster, which is officially marked on maps as Northern Ireland. There has been fighting here on and off and on again for more than eight hundred years. Some of the worst of the fighting has been in the last thirty years. These times since 1968 are known as the Troubles, and they are all the children here have ever known.

What is it about Ulster? The story began so long ago, when there was no Northern Ireland, no divided country—only one Ireland. The people of this island were known as the Celts. They settled in Ireland around 350 B.C. Theirs was a rich culture, organized into clans and governed by a highly organized set of laws known as the Brehon Law. The Celts paid great honor to poets and storytellers and were known as well for the fierceness of their warriors and the constant warfare between the clans.

The island was divided into four great kingdoms: Ulster, Leinster, Munster, and Connaught. Ulster, the farthest north, consisted of nine counties stretching across Ireland, from sea to sea. At the easternmost point of land, the water dividing Ireland from Scotland is less than twenty miles wide. That closeness is an important part of the story.

THE FOUR KINGDOMS

ULSTER

CONNAUGHT

LEINSTER

MUNSTER

Around the year 1170 the king of England, Henry II, declared himself king of Ireland as well. Gradually, with great bloodshed, Ireland was brought under the control of England, or Great Britain, as England came to be known. Through the centuries, Ireland was held as a colony of the British Empire—held against the wishes of the Irish people.

There were also other people living in Ireland, however. English settlers had been going to Ireland for centuries, and beginning in 1609 James I, then king of England, offered land to Scottish settlers if they would move to Ireland and farm the land—land that was being taken from the native Irish.

To the Irish, these new arrivals came to be known as the strangers: people with a different language, a different way of life, and, most important, a different religion. For the people of Ireland were Catholic and the strangers taking over their land were Protestant. At that time in England and in much of Europe, a terrible intolerance existed between different religions.

The English gradually put laws into place that said Catholics could not own land, could not vote, could not be elected to public office or work for the government. Catholics were not allowed to be lawyers. They were not allowed to speak the Irish

language or study Irish history or literature. They were forbidden to hold Mass. Bishops, priests, and monks were forced to leave the country. By 1780 the Irish people owned only five percent of their own land, and in 1800 the British government passed the Act of Union, declaring Ireland part of the United Kingdom of Great Britain and Ireland.

Through the long years of British rule, the Irish fought for their freedom. They fought with what weapons they had, in rebellions great and small—rebellions that the vast British army always put down. The Irish fought with words as well as weapons. They organized and signed petitions, held massive nonviolent protests, and after Catholics regained the vote in 1829, they lobbied in the English Parliament for their freedom.

In 1916, during World War I, a small rebellion broke out in

Dublin on Easter Monday. The Irish rebels were quickly defeated. Sixteen of the leaders were shot, and many men and women were jailed, including some who had not been involved. Anger grew in Ireland. People began to join Sinn Fein, a political group working for Irish freedom. In the Irish language,

Sinn Fein means "ourselves alone." Those who felt it was necessary to fight with weapons joined the IRA—the Irish Republican Army— and fought the British army where and when they could. The outnumbered IRA, led by a man named Michael Collins, managed to inflict losses on the superior British forces. The Irish people began to believe that this time would be different, this time freedom would finally come.

But the Protestants of Ireland did not approve of the rebellion. They had lived in Ireland for generations. They owned land and businesses. And they knew who they were: They were British subjects, and they believed Ireland should remain part of the United Kingdom. They were willing to fight to keep it so. "No surrender" became their motto. Great numbers of Protestants were living in the North; their cry was "Ulster will fight, and Ulster will be right."

The damages inflicted by the Irish rebels grew, and the British government agreed in 1920 to meet with the Irish for peace talks. After difficult negotiations, the British agreed to the Irish demands for self-government and freedom. But they did not agree to freedom for

all of Ireland. Ulster, where so many British Protestants lived, would become Northern Ireland and would become part of the United Kingdom of Great Britain and Northern Ireland. But not all of Ulster would become Northern Ireland. A new border would be drawn to create a place where there would be more Protestants than Catholics. Three counties—Donegal, Cavan,

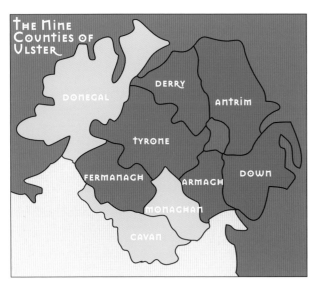

and Monaghan—of the original nine making up Ulster were not included in Northern Ireland. This was the deal the British offered. If it was not accepted, the talks would be ended, and the fighting would begin again.

In Ireland, the arguments over the proposal were fierce. Some believed there should be no division of the country—no deal. Others thought it was the best deal possible at that time. They believed that creating Northern Ireland was a temporary measure and Ireland would soon be reunited. In the end, Ireland took the offer. But anger over the division of the country was so strong that civil war broke out. Friends who had fought together against the British now turned on one another.

And so in 1921, while most of the Irish gained their freedom, the Catholics of Northern Ireland remained under British rule. In the new Ulster, Catholics could not vote unless they owned land, and few did. Businesses, government, public housing, and jobs were all controlled by Protestants.

In 1968, Catholics began to form civil rights organizations, inspired by the work of people like Dr. Martin Luther King Jr. in the United States. Catholics wanted to have the same rights as Protestants. They began a series of protest marches across Northern Ireland. The government forbade the marches. Catholic demonstrators were attacked and gassed. Catholic homes, neighborhoods, and churches were attacked by mobs who believed that the Catholics were not entitled to equal rights.

The Catholics began to fight back, arming themselves. The Irish Republican Army, whose numbers had dwindled since the country was divided, gained new recruits and became active again. The British army moved in to try to stop the fighting, but the battles grew worse. After fourteen unarmed protesters were killed by a British army regiment in 1972, on a day that became known as Bloody Sunday, the IRA's membership swelled. Soon the cities and towns of Northern Ireland were battlegrounds.

Both the Protestants and the Catholics made bombs, blew up buildings, and created armies. The IRA began to argue within its ranks about tactics, splitting into different groups.

One group, called the Provisional IRA, or "the Provos," became the present-day IRA. Both Catholics and Protestants were guilty of murder and mayhem. At one point there were as many as seven armed groups on the streets of Belfast. Even the question of civil rights seemed to have been lost amidst the violence and the constant calls for revenge.

More than 3,200 people have died in the Troubles—men, women, and children—Protestant and Catholic alike. They died over the question "Are we British or are we Irish?" And after all this time, there are still two very different answers to that question. The deaths have not changed this.

The habit of hating is a hard one to break. But many people believe it is worth a try. People on both sides of the walls who want peace keep working to stop the fighting. In 1997, a new cease-fire went into effect. Peace talks began, which led to the signing of a peace accord in 1998. A new government for North-

ern Ireland was formed, intending to guarantee the rights of Catholics.

But as the song says, what about Ulster? No one knows the answer. Some say there will be no peace until the entire island of Ireland is united. Some say there will be no peace if that ever happens.

Through all the fighting, the people of Belfast have been living their lives. Children of both sides have gone to school, though never with one another. They've played soccer, ridden bicycles, thrown rocks, and teased their friends. They've had dreams, the same as kids everywhere—to be famous, to be soccer players, to be rock stars. Some have gotten into trouble, for there's trouble around to be had. Some have taken up the fight, picked up the gun. Some have searched for another way. For, though they have known nothing but the Troubles, they have their hopes, they make their plans.

A NEW STORY

Liam Leathem walks through the winter light of his neighborhood, Turf Lodge, in the city of Belfast, Northern Ireland. He pulls on his blue stocking cap, the one he always wears, cold or no. Up ahead he spots a group of kids younger than his eleven years. The gang is throwing rocks at a wall, a wall covered with words. The graffiti proclaims WE SHALL NEVER BE DEFEATED. Other slogans read IRA and TIOCFAIDH ÁR LA. All the rock throwers, whether they speak Irish or not, know that these last words proclaim OUR DAY WILL COME.

One girl climbs high up on the wall, balancing on the very top. *She'll catch it*, Liam thinks, *if her mam sees.* Liam listens as the girl tells the others something not written on the wall.

"Eamon loves Orla. Eamon loves Orla . . ." she chants, and the others join in. All the others, that is, except Eamon and Orla. A gang of bigger boys, waiting on the opposite corner for trouble to come their way, begin to laugh. The little kids are not afraid of the big ones, for they are all from the same neighborhood, all Catholic.

Liam hears the sound of a car driving too fast through the narrow streets.

"Joy riders!" someone screams as everybody steps out of the street to safety. The stolen car, speeding, might come this way.

"Hey, where you going, Rocky?" the high-climbing, cheeky girl asks as Liam passes by.

Liam smiles. "Where do you think?" he tells her, walking on. Behind him the song changes from one about who loves whom to a song from the streets of Turf Lodge.

"What about Ulster?" sings someone, probably Eamon, quite loudly.

"What about Sinn Fein?" another responds.

"What about Allied Carpet?" the whole group proclaims.

"Do you think it will be bombed again?" Liam adds his own voice to the last line as he passes the big lads.

"Where are you going, Rocky?" asks the shortest, his hands cupped carefully round a cigarette.

"Where do you think?" Liam answers, not meaning any trouble.

Before the short smoker can decide what he thinks, an almighty bang is heard from the street up the hill.

"Crash!" cries the girl high up on the wall.

"Bomb!" Someone offers another opinion. Legs long and short set off running up the street toward the noise.

Liam, hands in his pockets, continues quietly in the other direction. He heads toward a plain, square building next to the Holy Trinity Church. A boy comes running out from a side alley, almost smashing into Liam.

"Bomb or crash, Rocky?" he asks, continuing on so fast that he couldn't hear the answer even if Liam had one.

What about Turf Lodge? That's what the song should say, Liam thinks. *There is always something happening here. Always something.*

Entering the Holy Trinity Boxing Club, Liam blinks his eyes at the great change from the gray light outside. High ceiling lights are on at full brightness. Everywhere, color greets the eye. The walls are deep green, the boxing mats a strong red, as are the gloves the boxers wear. Posters cover the walls top to bottom—famous boxers, famous places around the world, newspaper stories about local boxers and lists of exercises for the boxers to do in the gym.

Liam looks again at the photos of winning boxers. Only four more days until his big fight on Monday. He knows he must train hard, every day, to win. And win is what Liam wants to do. Monday night will be the County Antrim championships. A win there and Liam will be off to fight in Dublin, in the south. *So get to work*, he tells himself.

The posters and the newspaper clippings hold Liam's attention while "What about Ulster?" bangs around in his brain. A yellowing newspaper article shows his coach, Mickey

SUNDAY MORNING
WARM UP   5 MIN
STRETCH   5 MIN
SPARRING 3×3=12 MIN
SHADOW BOX 2×3= 8 MIN
PADWORK 2×3= 8 MIN
BAGWORK 4×3=16 MIN
SKIPPING ROPE 4×3=16 MIN
GENERAL EX.   15 MIN
STRETCH   5 MIN
WARM DOWN   5 MIN
TRAINING NEXT WEEK
SAME TIME.
        TOTAL TIME 110 MIN

Hawkins, walking in an Olympic parade. Mickey was once a boy in Turf Lodge, the same as Liam. Other grainy pictures show young champions lined up, looking tough and pleased. Liam spies a photo of his other coach, Tony Leonard, taken years ago when he won a championship fight.

Soon they'll be writing and talking about Liam "Rocky" Leathem, Liam thinks. *Liam, champion of the world.*

Words drift into the club along with the boxers big and small who come to train there.

"Crash up the hill!" someone announces.

"Joy rider hit a black taxi!" says someone else who sounds like he knows for sure.

"No one hurt, but the rider ran off." Another boy states the details.

"He better run from the Ra," comments another, referring to the Provos.

"Not a bomb?"

"Sure there is a cease-fire. Why would there be a bomb?"

"Sure cease-fires are made to be broken."

Liam listens to the words, to the everyday greetings from his boxing mates. But he keeps jumping rope, warming up. He knows he cannot answer the song's question, "What about Ulster?" But what about Liam? Ah, he knows the answer to that one. Liam wants to do his fighting in a ring. He wants to win, he does not care if the other boxer is Catholic or not. He wants to go all around the world, to all the places on the posters, to all the places his coaches have seen. And Liam will be happy to start with Dublin. So he pulls on the red gloves and with all his might he punches a large black bag hanging down from the ceiling. It moves not a whit.

Around the gym, the noise grows. Gloves make contact with bags, with other gloves. Ropes slap against mats. Boxers grunt as they practice. Coaches call out instructions as rock music blares from a radio. The singer cries out "Bang, bang," seeming to keep time with Liam's gloves going *bang bang* against the unmoving black bag.

Mickey Hawkins carefully checks Liam's headgear. No boy is allowed to box without his head and mouth protected, whether in practice or in matches.

"Come on, Rocky, show me what you can do," Mickey challenges Liam. The other kids in Turf Lodge started calling Liam "Rocky" when he began to win the local fights. The name stuck.

"Come on now," Mickey says as he circles away, hands held high. Liam holds his hands up, feet dancing on the mat, waiting. He takes a punch.

"What are you doing now, swimming?" Mickey asks. "No swimming. Arms short and tight, with speed."

Liam tries hard to think all at once about where his hands, feet, and head should be. Mickey cries out "Ah!" over and over again as—*whap, whap*—Liam's gloves connect. Liam exhales noisily. "Pah, pah, pah," Mickey says as Liam gets the rhythm right and "Well done lad," when the sparring is done. Liam hands his gloves to the next boxer, for there are not enough to go around. Mickey smiles, pulling Liam's hand into the air: "Winner and still champion!"

Liam rests awhile as he watches his friend Peter jump

rope. Winner and still champion. Those words will be said about Liam for real someday. And so, tired as he is, he trains some more. *Whap, whap,* he hits the black bag. "Ah, ah," Mickey urges the boy in the ring. "Bang, bang" goes the radio. Just a song, not a bomb.

☩HE air is cool on Liam's sweaty head as he leaves the gym with his mates. Peter and then Gerard turn off at their homes, and Liam is left walking alone. The houses he passes all look the same, one street after another. As he walks, Liam passes the spot where a bus was burned not so long ago. A riot had broken out when a British soldier convicted of shooting a joy rider was released from prison. Liam passes a wall where a boy from Turf Lodge was killed when he was hit by a rubber bullet. The army said he was rioting. His family knows he was not. Liam was born after this happened, but like every other child in Belfast, Catholic or Protestant, he knows the stories, passed on, told over and again.

Liam punches his hands back and forth in the air as he comes to his house. Inside he finds everyone watching a football match between the Glasgow Celtics and the Glasgow Rangers. "Football" is what soccer is known as

in Belfast. Liam's parents, Bridie and Peter, and his brothers, Peter Jr. and Michael, are gathered around the television.

"Who is winning?" Liam asks, finding himself the arm of a chair.

"We are, by one goal," says Peter, who is fourteen.

"Training go all right?" Liam's mother wants to know.

"Oh, aye," Liam answers, keeping his eye on the Celtics as they try for another goal. In Belfast, Catholics cheer for the Celtics; Protestants root for the Rangers. It is that simple. Woe to anyone seen wearing the colors of one in the neighborhood of the other.

"I'm off," young Peter says, heading to his room to listen to music. Peter much prefers music to sports. This frustrates Liam, who prefers sports to almost anything.

"I'm reading the dictionary," six-year-old Michael tells Liam.

"How can you read when your eyes are too close together?" Liam teases him.

"They are not so!" Michael cries.

"Ah, leave him," Bridie chides Liam as he begins to measure the space between his own eyes and then Michael's.

In a recent television program about the Troubles, the Leathems had listened as a reporter asked some Protestant children if they knew any Catholics.

"No, we do not," a boy had answered for them all. "But if we did, we would throw rocks at them."

"Why?" the reporter had wondered.

"Because they are Catholics" was given as reason enough.

When asked how they would know they were Catholics, everyone answered, "Sure, Catholics' eyes are too close together."

When Catholic children were asked if they would throw stones at the Protestants, they all answered, "We must. For they might throw stones at us!"

"And round and round it goes," Liam's father had summed it up.

Later, Liam and Michael had examined their eyes in the mirror. Liam crossed his eyes to see how he might look if they really were too close together. Michael assured him that he looked none too good. "Ah, *I* would throw stones at you if you looked like that!"

That same night in bed, Liam could not turn off his thinking. He

knew his eyes were just where they should be. *I'm Rocky*, he thought to himself. He knew those other lads didn't care. To them, he was simply someone to throw rocks at.

B**ut** tonight Liam works on his homework on the sitting room floor. His mind is in the boxing club, not here at home.

"Can you give me some words from that dictionary?" Liam asks Michael. "I have to write a poem for school and I have no words."

"Why not?" his father asks.

"Dunno," answers Liam.

"You say that a lot," his father comments.

Finally Liam says, looking up at his mother, "Listen to this one." Michael pauses to listen as well.

> I am a tank. I have a machine gun.
> Bang bang bang. I kill a wee nun.

There is silence in the room for a moment after Liam is finished.

"Well, it's very Belfast," his father notes.

"Do I know this nun, Liam?" Michael wants to know.

Later, Michael falls asleep worrying about the nun. Liam forgets about the poem and falls asleep while mentally practicing his moves. *Pah, pah. Only three more days and it will be Monday. Monday when they'll be too busy watching my fists fly to bother looking at me eyes.*

B**EFORE** leaving for school the next morning, Liam brings his mother a cup of morning tea. Cups of tea are made, poured, and drunk all day in the Leathem house.

"Cheerio," Liam calls as he goes.

"Mind the tanks and nuns," Bridie calls after him.

As the three brothers leave the house, Peter turns left and Michael and Liam turn right. Peter leaps a fence, making his way through a trash-strewn field, finally squeezing through a hole in the large steel fence that surrounds Turf Lodge. One after another of his mates follow the same route, heading along the motorway to the Christian Brother's Secondary School. Next year Liam will join the fence-squeezers.

But for now the two younger brothers head up the street in the opposite direction from Peter. On the corner where last night's crash occurred, they see two boys and a girl picking up stray bits of brightly colored glass. Liam

had seen this same girl balancing high on a fence last night. "She is going to catch it, that one," Liam tells Michael.

The path to the school leads uphill. The Holy Trinity School for Boys sits on one of the highest points in Turf Lodge, at the very edge of the neighborhood. The Black Mountain, Belfast's great hill, looms over the school.

As gangs of kids approach the school, the girls peel off to the lower

building, the Holy Trinity School for Girls. In Belfast, girls and boys go to separate schools, as do Catholics and Protestants.

Behind Liam's school, a soccer game is in full swing. The biggest boys play a game that ranges from one end of the playing field to the other. Great gobs of younger boys run in all directions. The youngest boys watch in groups, not sure how to get in the game, till a gang of them runs over and jumps on the goalie.

"Oh no, it's the little ones!" the goalie yells. Laughing, he fends off the attack. A boy named John Paul in honor of the pope cannot play, for he broke his arm. His mate has to watch as well, since he has only one pair of shoes. His mother would fair kill him if he ruined them.

Liam loves the running, the game, the early morning. Even the noise of the ever-present army helicopter flying overhead and taking pictures bothers him not at all. The bell rings, but no one wants to go in. One boy, clutching his soccer ball, pleads for more time. His teacher thinks he should go in now. Liam heads inside, but he wishes he could keep running—outside of Turf Lodge, down the motorway. He would like to run so hard and so far that he would reach the top of Black Mountain. But Liam hardly ever leaves Turf Lodge. *Stay where you are known, where it is safe*—this is the unwritten rule that Liam and all the children of Belfast learn early.

But I'll leave here soon enough, Liam thinks. *A win on Monday night, and it's off to Dublin for me.*

T**HE** students, big and small, file into the bare room that doubles as a gym and an assembly hall. Liam's class, the "big men" of the school at eleven, fill in the back wall. Waiting for the younger ones to take their places, Liam reads the work hanging on the wall. Large construction-paper letters spell the words WE ARE SORRY and SHOWING LOVE. Some of the lower-grade students have drawn pictures and written words to illustrate these ideas.

I DO NOT SHOW LOVE WHEN I AM BOLD IN CLASS declares one writer. I DO NOT SHOW LOVE WHEN I KICK OTHER PEOPLE AND THROW BIG THINGS AT THEM says another. *Ah well, he has the idea,* Liam thinks as he tries to keep a straight face.

Mr. Hutton, the school principal, strides in. He leads the boys in prayers that they all know. "Our Father who art in Heaven," say the voices all together. "Holy Mary, Mother of God, pray for us sinners," everyone intones. Liam wonders if the boy who kicks and throws big things is right now asking for special help.

Mr. Hutton announces there will be awards given this morning. He's a great man for handing out prizes. But first Mr. Hutton leads the school in learning a new hymn for St. Patrick's Day Mass. He sings a line; the boys repeat. And then again, till they all sing in one voice from beginning to end:

> Dear Glorious Saint Patrick, Dear Saint of our Isle,
> On us thy poor children, bestow a sweet smile,
> And though thou art high in the mansions above,
> On Erin's green valleys look down with thy love.

A simple song, lovely with all the boys' voices singing together. A simple song that declares, *We are all Irish here*, that this city of Belfast is part of the whole island of Ireland. A simple song that asks the patron saint of the Irish nation to look down with care on the children of Turf Lodge. A song only to be sung in a Catholic school in a Catholic neighborhood, or woe betide the singer.

"Well done," Mr. Hutton confirms when the song is learned. "Today we are awarding certificates to boys whose work has shown great improvement." He starts to call out names, beginning with the youngest. Brendan is called, then Sean. Dermot, Conor, Danny, Diarmuid, Aidan, and Eamon. Liam looks up to read the papers again: I DO NOT SHOW LOVE WHEN I CALL MY CLASSMATES NAMES I CANNOT WRITE HERE, an hon-

est boy has written. Liam, busy sti-fling a laugh, does not hear his own name called.

"Rocky, it's you," hisses a classmate.

"Liam Leathem," Mr. Hutton an-nounces for the second time.

Liam makes haste to the front of the classroom. Accepting Mr. Hut-ton's handshake, Liam thinks, *I do not show love when I do not pay attention in assembly.*

In the classroom, Mr. Armstrong

sorts out the day's business. "Right, now I need a volunteer to do the mission money. Who's a good lad?"

He glares at them with his friendly glare, not his serious one. All the boys know and respect the difference. "Ah, and who is going to take on the terrible chore of getting lunch tickets for me?"

All hands fly into the air, and Liam nearly jumps out of his chair. "All right then," Mr. Armstrong says, choosing Liam. "But no stopping to put on after-shave along the way," he says as Liam leaves to the hoots of his classmates. Each one wishes he was going to pick up the tickets from Mr. Hutton's secretary. They all think she is brilliant-looking.

The day passes with schoolwork. In math, the boys count and sort by type the vehicles that pass over the motorway outside the classroom window. An argument breaks out over whether armored cars and army trucks are in the same category or two different ones. And then there is the question of taxis. Do the black taxis, run by the IRA to make money, count as regular taxis? This leads to a discussion of the crash the night before:

who saw it, who thinks he knows what. The one thing on which everyone agrees is that the joy rider may be in danger. If the IRA finds out who he is, there will be a beating, a punishment to discourage others.

The morning soccer game continues at lunch while an army helicopter hovers overhead. A few boys yell rude things to the soldiers. Most ignore them. The sound of helicopters flying overhead is an everyday sound in Belfast.

At the end of the day, Mr. Armstrong begins to assign roles for the Easter play. Written by Mr. Armstrong and Mr. Harte, the vice principal, the play shows Christ's journey to his crucifixion. Intermixed in the play are scenes from today's news that show lessons still to be learned from Jesus.

Someone must be chosen to play Jesus carrying the cross, someone who will not disgrace the part. Everyone wants the role, including Liam. Red-haired Robert with glasses and good grades wins the part. Robert practices

hanging on the cross while Mr. Armstrong goes over the play. Liam wonders if there might be a part for a boxer who uses his talents to defend Jesus.

Liam's mind wanders to the fight on Monday. Keeping his hands below the desk, he practices short and tight, no swimming. *The fight is coming; be ready,* he tells himself. Outside the window, he spies soldiers running at a fast trot along the hill. *What's up there?* Liam wonders for barely a moment. The sound of helicopters grows louder, competing with Mr. Armstrong's plenty-strong voice. The end-of-school bell rings, adding to the noise.

As Liam leaves the school, he sees more than the usual single helicopter overhead. As the boys file down the hill in a neat, orderly line, armored cars race along up the road behind them.

"Fight!" someone yells as they reach the end of the school property. A great gang runs off to watch and cheer.

"A bomb!" shouts another, pointing to the helicopters, passing on the news.

Liam corrals Michael. "If we hurry home, we can go meet Dad at Granddad's. Come on, I want to help feed the pigeons."

"I want to go and see the bomb," Michael complains.

"There's no bomb," Liam says. "There's a cease-fire."

"Cease-fires are made to be broken. Everyone says so." Michael insists.

"If there is fighting to be done around here, I'll do it," Liam tells Michael.

"Watch this." As they walk, Liam practices short and fast. Michael loses

interest in the bomb, telling Liam a story he learned in school, about a man who climbed a tree to see Jesus.

"Did Jesus have red hair and glasses?" Liam asks.

"I don't think we were told," says Michael, seeming worried not to know.

They head home as a soldier patrol passes in the other direction.

"**H**ERE'S my dad," Liam says as he greets his father and his grandfather. Behind his grandfather's house, the two men are fussing with their pigeons in the coop. Liam goes to help while Michael heads inside with his Aunt Bernie, looking for sweets.

"Bomb went off in Ballymurphy," Liam's dad tells him.

"Can I feed the pigeons?" Liam asks.

"First let them out. They'll come back for the food," his father chides.

The pigeons fly up high and around. Wings flap loudly, a new sound added to the constant helicopter noise. Liam leans his head back to watch them.

"Could they fly round the world?" Liam asks, wondering.

"Sure not, but they do fly back from France in the races," his granddad answers.

"I used to know a man who won that race," his father says. "A good man, a Protestant man. And now I wouldn't know how to find his house, what with peace walls in the way."

Liam has a thought: "The birds could go see your man, couldn't they?"

"Oh aye, they can, but I can't," Liam's dad says. Liam realizes that he

himself does not know even one Protestant. He may have passed one on a neutral street, perhaps in the city center, but he has never really met a Protestant boy except to fight one in the boxing ring.

Liam wonders if the pigeons of Turf Lodge, flying about, meet the pigeons of the good Protestant man. What do they do? Ignore each other? Fight each other? Maybe the pigeons get along famously, passing on news of garbage dumps to visit and helicopters to watch out for.

"Time now," says Liam's dad. So Liam shakes the food to bring the birds home.

LATER on, it is back to the gym for Liam. Past the big lads congregating once more. "Where are you going, Rocky?" comes the question again. Liam waves, passing by. This night a few of the boys peel off from the gang, following Liam to the gym door.

"Going to fight, Rocky, are you?" one calls out as they come closer, but not so friendly.

Mickey Hawkins comes along as Liam does. He notices the lads, has seen this game before. "In you go, Liam," he tells him. "Off you go," he says to the others.

Inside the gym, cables cover the floor. "Radio!" Liam's mate Peter calls excitedly.

Right then two boxers arrive. They train in this gym, and tomorrow they will be off for a big tournament down in Dublin. Everyone around Turf Lodge knows these two are the best in all of Ireland. Now they are going down south to prove it.

The radio man interviews the boxers, holding a microphone close so each of them can answer. Liam cannot help himself—he moves closer and closer still, till he almost trips over the cable and into the radio man from Dublin.

"Easy now. Back away, lad," warns a man with earphones on his head.

Liam moves away, thinking, *Someday soon, you'll be coming back to interview me.* He pulls on a pair of gloves, getting ready for that someday. Later, he poses with the two famous boxers, looking as serious as he can.

On Saturday, Liam rises early. While his dad leaves to take care of his pigeons, Liam sets out on a training run. No lazy morning. Two more days to go.

Today, Liam's cousin Ryan and his boxing mate Gerard come along. The morning is cold, but the sun warms them. They move through the streets of

Turf Lodge to the Falls Road Park, through the Catholic part of West Belfast. It's perfectly safe for these three boys. They end their run across from Milltown Cemetery. The old Irish crosses, Celtic crosses, show this to be a Catholic cemetery, as do the graves of IRA men and women.

A hearse drives in slowly, followed in the Irish way by mourners on foot. Across the street, surrounded by metal walls and wire mesh, an army observation tower looks down on the quiet morning scene.

Every Saturday afternoon, Liam, Michael, and often Ryan head to the movies. Always to the same movie theater, upstairs from the shops. The movie is filled with neighborhood kids along with one teenage boy whose job it is to keep order. On their morning run, Liam and Ryan had hatched a plan. "Please, Da." Liam gives it a try when he gets home. "Please let us go to the other movie theater."

A new place has opened. The boys have heard reports of big seats that lean back with holders on the sides for drinks. They are itching to see if this is true and also to see the new action movie that is showing there and nowhere else.

"I'm not taking you there. No. Subject closed," Liam's dad declares as he cooks up an Ulster fry for his family, which he does every Saturday. An Ulster fry is made up of fried eggs, fried potatoes, fried bread, and fried sausages. "My granddad, who gave me my pigeons, had an Ulster fry every day of his life, and two on Saturday," he says to change the subject, nodding toward the picture of his granddad on the wall.

"He did, for true," Liam's mother testifies as she makes the tea. "Only he never called this Ulster. This was always the Six Counties, to him."

"After all, he fought with Michael Collins," Liam's dad says.

"So he did," young Peter agrees, picking up a cup of tea on his way back to his room, the music playing loudly.

"Please, Da." Liam tries to turn the subject back again. "It is supposed to be brilliant."

"It's brilliant, is it? And what road is it at the end of?" Liam's dad asks. "And who is living on that road. Protestants, are they not? And what is going to happen to you when the lads in the movie theater discover the Turf Lodge Three sitting among them with mouths full of sweets?"

"I dunno," Liam tries.

"Well, I do know, and you are not going," the boys' father finishes.

"I can take them on," Liam offers, putting up his fists.

"So, Superman, you can take on a whole movie theater and watch out for Michael as well?"

"Ah, no," Liam admits defeat.

And so it is off to the same old movie theater,

to where they are known—where boys and girls from Holy Trinity run up and down the aisle, eat too many sweets, annoy the movie monitor, listen to a girl named Orla say loudly who she does not love, and ponder the question Michael asks everyone: Did Jesus have red hair and glasses?

Sunday passes quietly, as Sundays do. Liam would spend the whole day at the boxing club except that no one thinks that is a good idea. No one but Liam. He heads outside to play soccer by himself; his brothers will not come along. Liam tells them exactly how pathetic they are for not joining in. He gets some words from his father for doing so.

Outside by himself, Liam plays a championship game. He kicks the ball, scoring goal after goal, hearing the roar of the invisible crowd. As Liam accepts a

standing ovation, the soldiers come round the corner, heading toward him. Liam wonders what he looks like to them, as they eye him down the barrels of their guns.

All weekend the grown-up talk has been about the peace accord. Will the cease-fire hold? A Catholic taxi driver was murdered the other day. Will a Protestant be shot in return? It seems as if the city is always holding its breath, waiting to see what will happen next.

Stepping to the side, holding his ball till the soldiers pass, Liam wishes they would simply go away. He wants to think about his fight, wants the talk to be about Liam Leathem, winner and still champion. But with a bomb in Ballymurphy, Liam knows, the soldiers may not be going anywhere very soon.

WHEN Liam reaches the club on Sunday night, he finds some of the street corner lads waiting for him outside the gym. The biggest lad blocks the door.

"Where are you going, Rocky?" he asks. Before Liam can answer, Mickey Hawkins is behind the big lad and in charge.

"Into the ring, Rocky," Mickey tells Liam. Then, looking at the others, he asks them a question. "Who wants to go a round with Rocky?" When none of them volunteers, Mickey chooses. "You then, how about you?"

The biggest boy soon finds himself in the ring, listening to the cheers and jeers of his mates. Liam faces his opponent on his own turf. *He's a big one*, Liam thinks, taking the measure of him. *But I know a few things he does not.*

Liam moves with the speed his coaches have taught him. Each time the bigger boy swings, Liam ducks, moves away, and is gone. The lad cannot find Liam with his gloves. "Come on, there's your man!" his friends call. But when the boy turns, Liam is gone. Then Liam swings, once and again, connecting both times, which makes the boy swing harder, wider, wilder.

No swimming now, Liam silently warns the boy. *Fast and tight.*

The street corner lads switch sides. Now Liam is their man. They shout "Rocky!" as Liam dances around, clearly in charge.

Mickey stops the fight with a quiet "That'll do now." The boy shakes Liam's gloved hand, smiling in defeat.

"All's well then," Mickey says. Now the lads have seen that they can either box or leave the boxers alone.

In the ring again, Mickey advises Liam, "Your man tomorrow will know how to box. Now show me you have not forgotten all I taught."

So around they go. A boxer's son, his pajamas as red as the boxing mat, watches carefully. "Me, me!" he calls out, wanting his turn.

"Tomorrow, then," Mickey says.

Liam nods as he heads home.

Liam has one more task this Sunday. The tank poem was none too successful at school. Making a space at the table, Liam tries again. He has an idea. Writing, erasing, Liam gets the words to go where he wants.

"Listen to my poem," he says to his family.

Bridie puts on her serious face for the listening.

Liam begins:

> I am a boxer, I fight all day.
> I am the champion from the USA.
> I am the champion, that I do know.
> My next fight is for the WBO.
> All those champions come and go
> But my name is Liam
> And I will never go.
> I will stay until the day
> That I decide to go.

Liam pauses, announcing, "The end."

"It's very good," Bridie assures Liam. "Much better than the wee nun."

"Why the USA?" his brother Peter asks.

"I dunno. It rhymes," Liam admits.

"Liam's from America?" Michael is surprised to find out.

"He dunno," his dad answers.

Sᴄʜᴏᴏʟ the next morning is spent rehearsing the play, though Liam has a hard time concentrating, as does the rest of the class. The rehearsal does not go well. Everyone but Robert has several parts to play, and no one seems to remember what he was told on Friday.

"Are ye Pontius Pilate, or are ye not?" Mr. Armstrong asks one boy, frustrated. "Where are my Protestants, where are ye?"

Liam and three other boys take their places. They play a Protestant family

forced to leave their home in a Catholic neighborhood. The other boys do a grand job of jeering, fists raised, faces hard. Liam knows that if this really happened to him, he would rather fight back than walk quietly through a mob. But that is not what the play says to do. One

boy does not want to play a Protestant. Liam pretends to be his father's friend, the good man with the pigeons. He tries to look as though he thinks all these yelling people have eyes that are too close together.

Robert hauls his cross around while Mr. Armstrong reads the narration.

"Now, where is my sad boy? Ah, great, there you go." He speaks encouragingly. The whole class admires Stephen, who does brilliant grief. In this scene, Stephen turns away from a toy store filled with toys he cannot have, his body bent, hand to head, shuffling slowly. The boy's father has no work, so the family has no money. Most of the boys in this room, including Liam, know this feeling. Jobs in Belfast are hard to come by for everyone.

"Now, where are my dead bodies? I need dead Bosnians," Mr. Armstrong demands. The bomb victims arrange themselves on the floor, Liam among them. Stephen does his grief again, this time playing a Bosnian mother who finds the bodies. "Great. Grand," says Mr. Armstrong.

Finally, the day is over. Liam hurries home. He needs to meet Mickey Hawkins at the club for a ride to the tournament.

Liam's mother takes the boxing charm from round Liam's neck. "Be careful, son," she cautions.

"Just listen to Mickey," his dad insists.

"Nervous?" Mickey asks Liam as he climbs into the car.

"No sir. I don't get nervous," Liam answers. *That is the truth*, Liam realizes. *I like to box, so I want to box, so I want to win. No reason to be nervous.*

The County Antrim championships are held in the Balmoral Hotel, across the city.

Liam watches as they travel up the Falls Road, past the Sinn Fein offices surrounded by high security wire, past a store with great stones in front to keep cars or bombs from crashing in. They move from a Catholic neighborhood into a Protestant one, the colors all around changing from the orange, green, and white of the Irish flag to the red, white, and blue of the British one.

Liam has been to the Balmoral Hotel once before, for lunch with Aunt Bernie on his confirmation day. The hotel hums with excitement, chock-a-block with people: boxers, their coaches, boxing fans, and those boxers' families who can afford to come. The ballroom where the fights will take place is filling up with both Catholics and Protestants come to cheer on their clubs. Everyone is polite. This evening is for boxing, not for trouble.

Liam goes downstairs to change into a club uniform. He gets his helmet and gloves ready. All the boys are buzzing about a boxer who has a bandage on his arm. The judges have checked underneath to make sure he is well enough to box. They found the words KILL ALL TAIGS tattooed on his arm. "Taig" is an insulting word used by some Protestants to describe Catholics.

"Same back to him!" a Turf Lodge boy declares. But Liam does not want to think about that boy or his tattoo. He does not want to beat his opponent because of someone's insulting words, or because the boy is Protestant. He wants to be winner and still champion. It is that simple. It does not matter who is in the ring. Liam wants this to be his fight tonight. Not Belfast's.

"Rocky, your turn." Liam is ready when they call him. He heads up the stairs with Gerard,

through the crowded room, into the brightly lit ring. Liam sees everyone watching but is not bothered. The excitement is part of the fun.

His opponent waits in the ring. Liam heads for his own corner. Tony Leonard, one of Liam's coaches, is there beside him. Mickey Hawkins is watching, too. Liam listens as the announcer says the two boys' names, their clubs, their ages.

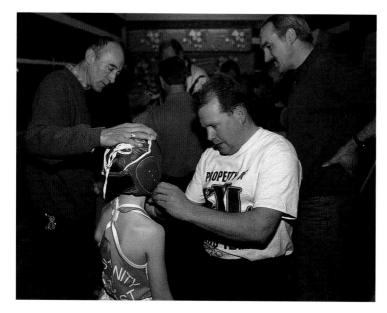

The boys come to center ring, the bell sounds, the match begins.

Liam shuffles his feet, the way he has been taught. His hands are up. Fast and quick, no swimming. His opponent has been told the same. The boy lands a punch, but Liam's helmet protects him. He dances away. Comes back. *Pah, pah.* Liam hits some. A bell rings, ending the first round. Both boys go to their corners.

"You're doing grand," Tony tells him. "I give that round to you." Liam agrees.

At Liam's level, a boxing match is three rounds long. Each round is one and one-half minutes. While the boys box, the three judges watch carefully, giving each boxer a score. The score is the judge's opinion of how well each boxer did. At the end, the scores are added up, and the boy with the most points wins.

The bell rings again. The second round begins. The boxers dance away from each other, come back together. Jab. Duck. Punch. Liam's glove connects with the boy's helmet once, and then again. The boy connects with Liam. Tight and fast, in and out again.

After the second round Tony says, "Well done."

I like this, Liam thinks. He believes he has done well.

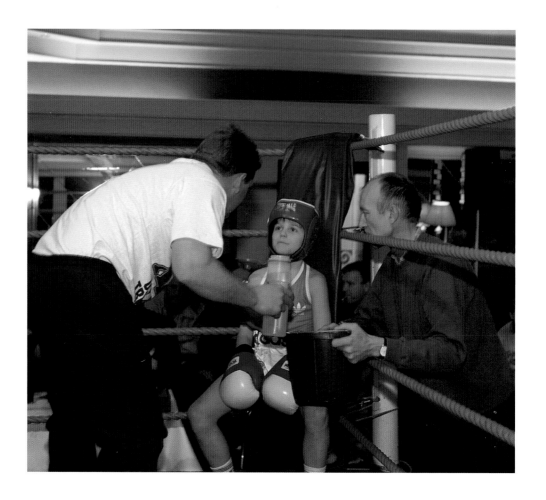

Another bell, another skirmish, till the last bell rings. Liam goes to his corner, takes off his helmet and boxing gloves. Then he and his coach shake hands with his opponent and the boy's coach. The boys go to the center to wait for the decision. They stand with the referee between them. Liam watches the judges. *I did well,* he thinks. *No swimming.*

Signaling that their decision has been reached, the judges call the referee. Both boxers hold their breath. The room is silent.

Standing between them, the referee pauses. He lifts the other boy's hand into the air. "The winner!"

Cheers come from one corner of the room. The winner exults. Other noises can be heard as well, complaining noises. Liam tries, hard as he can, to keep his feelings from his face. But the disappointment seeps through.

Liam felt sure he had won. But the three judges said not. As he walks

through the room, he keeps his head high. From more than one person he hears, "I thought you'd won."

As he changes out of his boxing clothes at the Balmoral and during the silent ride home, Liam plays the fight over and over again in his head. He agrees with everyone who thought he had won.

Did I lose because I'm from Turf Lodge? Because they think I'm a Taig whose eyes are too close together? Liam's anger begins to grow.

But then Liam remembers Mickey Hawkins's rule: "No one from our club is allowed to say they were robbed. No one. We win, or we lose. Then we go on."

Fair enough, decides Liam, his anger ebbing away. *I lost. This was my fight, no one else's. And I didn't win. But next time,* he tells himself, *next time, I will.*

⊙n a gray evening two nights later, Liam Leathem walks through the streets of Turf Lodge. The rock throwers are playing a mad game of football in the street, ignoring a passing army patrol that cannot ignore them. Everyone's head lifts up at the sound of screeching tires. Everyone judges the joy riders too far away to worry about.

The corner lads are there waiting, full of the talk. One lad swears he knows something about the bomb in Ballymurphy. The others listen, sure he does not. They all turn as Liam approaches.

"Did you win, Rocky?" the biggest lad asks. It's a friendly question.

"My fight? No, I did not," Liam tells them true.

"Will you fight again?"

"I will," Liam declares as he enters the gym.